The Essential Style Manual Narrated by: *The Well Appointed Gentleman*

ISBN: **1505368995**

ISBN-13: **978-1505368994**

DEDICATION

This manual is dedicated to my late father, Thomas E. Haynes Sr. He always supported everything that I dreamed, hoped, and wanted to be. He enjoyed dressing up when he had the chance and always admired my sense of style. Forever, you will always be my style inspiration!

CONTENTS

Published by Dr. Eduardo Haynes.

Edited by Danisha Ford
Cover designed, interior designed, illustrations and production coordinated by Dr. Eduardo Haynes

ACKNOWLEDGMENTS

I would like to thank everyone that has encouraged me to complete this journey of my life. I have grown to become a connoisseur of the art of curating pieces of clothing in my wardrobe to present the best version of myself. Dressing well is more than having style and keeping up with the latest trends. Every piece of clothing that I own in my wardrobe is an expression of my life and whom I choose to be regardless of my circumstances. I believe my talent and expertise are to be shared with any man who wishes to become a well-appointed gentleman.

1- THE WELL APPOINTED GENTLEMAN

The basis of this chapter is to share with you some insight into the background of The Well Appointed Gentleman. I remember as a young child before school began, my mother took me to New York to shop for clothes and shoes. She made my public appearance a priority, and she would not settle for less than exquisite apparel to include well-made garments. That was the time when I began my love affair with the art of dressing. I learned that dressing up is not the same as dressing well from within. To become a well-appointed gentleman, you must possess the skills to understand how manipulate material for the effect that you want to achieve. If you do not possess those skills, then self-expression is not possible.

My father was a blue-collar worker where he labored with his hands and did not wear white cuffs or collars. Instead, he wore casual dress clothing that was functional and did its job to protect him while he worked. On his days off from work, he dressed as a "gentleman" where his style in clothing reflected his selective taste and the pride he had in himself. His motto was, "A well-dressed man is a well-respected man". Often, I am reminded of the man my father was now that I have two sons of my own. My hope is to extend this legacy of being well-dressed as an important aspect of being a man.

Regardless of your financial situation, your size, or your height - your appearance gives a lasting impression. How you dress is more than just your appearance. Your appearance is a form of expression about who you are and how you feel about yourself. My hope in developing this guide is to inspire men to express their most positive qualities in any given situation. Each chapter provides a simple blueprint to my secrets of building a wardrobe with key pieces, tips, and tricks. You do not need to change your style of dress to improve your wardrobe. All you will need is to change the right things to simplify the art of dressing well, which is easier than you think. As you will see this in some of my selections and recommendations, I am a strict adherer of purchasing quality over quantity. This guide will illustrate how a well-dressed man can use his clothes to express the best version of self that he can be with a natural sense of style.

Be well, dress well, and be sure to shine your shoes! Enjoy the manual!

~ *The Well Appointed Gentleman*

2- THE WELL APPOINTED LIST

This chapter outlines some of the essential items that a gentleman needs to establish a solid wardrobe. Most importantly, keep in mind that the proper wardrobe must include essential pieces that you need ready in your closet. These items are the must haves, no matter what your style, that make up the basis of your wardrobe. The wardrobe essentials have several important attributes:

Mastering versatility

The secret of a well-dressed man is to purchase items that can be worn with everything you own. When you apply the rule of purchasing quality of quantity, your clothing is interchangeable with patterns that yield a higher return on your investment than any trendy piece that only matches one other piece in your wardrobe. Always apply the rule of quality over quantity because less truly is more.

Styles

Your appearance typically defines their demeanor and mood. Each person has their own style, which makes them unique. A well-dressed man has a wardrobe consisting of timeless pieces that are interchangeable. A well-dressed man's primary style of dress should be exemplary. However, a well-appointed gentleman's style requires consistency to remain open-minded and flexible. He must embrace the ability to mix patterns and colors with the knowledge that he takes risks to go against the norm for the sake of expressing his individuality.

Patterns

Some of the classic patterns include: pin stripes, checks, pin dots, argyle, tartan plaids, houndstooth, paisley, and the all time classic herringbone. These patterns can be found on suit fabrics, sport-coats, shirts, and ties. The more complicated patterns should be reserved as accent pieces such as ties, pocket squares, or socks. This is a way to have fun without breaking the bank.

Classic Colors

Without uttering a word, colors have powerful effects on our subconscious in every aspect of our lives. Colors stimulate our senses, which has an effect on the decisions we make when purchasing pieces. When adding essential pieces to your wardrobe, be aware of the impacts and responses of each color on your emotions. Not that any one color can be necessarily bad. Be mindful of the responses you want to receive as well as how you want to feel in your choice of colors. In addition, colors that compliment your complexion can be used to your advantage.

➢ *Red* – means energy, passion, action, strength, and excitement. It is best used as an accent color piece in your wardrobe for the action-oriented well-appointed gentleman who experience life through his five senses. This color is appropriate for the "power" tie in your collection but never a dress shirt!

➢ *Pink* – a sign of inspiration, hope, and reassurance for our future. This color worn by the well-appointed gentleman is accepted and unconditionally loved by others. Pink is one of the versatile shirt color and pairs well with blues and grays.

➢ *White* – a blank canvas that alleviates emotional upsets and creates a sense of order and efficiency if you need to purify your thoughts and spirit. White is worn mostly by a well-appointed gentleman who enjoys the simplicities of life. He portrays self-reliance and does not depend on others. Best worn when added to other appropriate colors to reflect individuality.

➢ *Orange* - means adventure, which inspires and creates enthusiasm in social communication. Also worn as an accent for the extroverted and sometimes flamboyant lighthearted and agreeable well-appointed gentleman who appreciates physical and social challenges.

➢ *Yellow* – means optimistic, uplifting and illuminating, brightening people's spirits. This color is for that well-appointed gentleman who utilizes his the logical side of his brain to inspire and create new ideas. Only use yellow to highlight another color, but do not use too much. The best use of this color is through a tie.

➢ *Green* – communicates balance and harmony of the mind, the body, and the emotions by creating a sense of calm. It assists in decision making by helping us to see all sides clearly. The color is worn by the well-appointed gentleman who appreciates the feeling of being safe and secure and being appreciated by others. Only wear one piece of this color, perhaps a silk knit tie!

➤ *Blue* – inspires integrity and honesty. A well-appointed gentleman who prefers this color also values inner peace and truth, and does not yield his perspectives of life to please others. You can never go wrong with the color blue; no matter what piece you wear.

➤ *Black* – implies self-control and discipline, and gives an impression of authority. However, a well-appointed gentleman who maintains power and control over their achievements and goals in life wears black with poise. The best use of this color is for a tuxedo!

➤ *Gray* – controlled color that balances and tones down stronger and brighter colors and illuminates the softer colors. Gray projects a well-appointed gentleman as cool, composed and reliable.

➤ *Lavender* – heightens sense of attractiveness and sophistication. A well-appointed gentleman who maintains emotional security and creates order and perfection favors wearing this color. He enjoys initiating and participating in humanitarian projects while helping others in need. Whatever purple particle you choose to wear, this color combines well with gold, turquoise, green, deep red and yellow. Blending this color with orange creates a contemporary look.

Top list of things that a true gentleman must OWN:

1. A Navy two-button sport-coat with side vents, surgeons cuff (working button holes on the sleeves), & ticket pocket- the navy sport-coat is versatile as it matches everything in your closet and is a staple. Whether it is jeans, trousers, or cords – the blazer will compliment it.

The surgeons cuff dates back to the days when doctors operated in blazers. The sleeves would have working buttonholes so that they could be rolled up during surgery. The modern take on this denotes "custom" or conversation piece. It also helps when you have a French cuff shirt or cufflinks that you want show off.

The history of the ticket pocket dates back to the time when gentleman would attend the opera and needed somewhere to place their ticket. Hence the word ticket pocket. This is a small pocket with a flap placed above the normal pockets on a sport-coat. This elevates the look of your outfit making you stand out against the rest wearing the "typical" blue sport-coat.

2. Seven pairs of shoes (Derby or Oxford, Monk Strap, Driver, Athletic Shoe, Loafer, Chukka & Dress Boot) these shoes will take you through all of the seasons, formal to casual, and work to play. Owning seven pairs of shoes keeps you from wearing out your collection. The shoe selection is the first thing that is noticed on a gentleman, so this needs special attention, and your dress shoes should be brown! Save the black for funerals and formal events!

3. Midnight blue Dinner Jacket – this can be the go to formal or dressed up date night piece. It can be paired with a tuxedo trouser or a pair of dark jeans for a Avant Garde appearance. Contrary to popular belief navy blue is the new black. Stand out against the crowd, break from the traditional black with a navy silhouette, and to punch it up another level – have one made in velvet!

4. Woven and Knit silk ties – the rationale for woven or knit ties is the weight. There is nothing worse than have a flimsy tie that makes a small knot. The heavier the fabric the better the knot and durability of the tie. Find patterns and colors that compliment your style.

5. Twelve dress shirts (White, Blue, Pink, & Lavender Solids; Blue stripe, check, & plaid) – These shirts pair best with gray or blue suits. They also create a professional and classic appearance that is a little different from the traditional white shirt. Yes, lavender is on the list of must have colors because it takes the tone of whatever tie and accessories that you are wearing. This sets you apart from everyone else in the office by creating a little visual interest.

6. A timepiece with a leather strap – Notice I did not say watch…A timepiece is something that you do not wear to the gym or cut the grass. It is meant to compliment your attire. Once you find a timepiece, you admire purchase additional leather straps so you can create interchangeable looks and interest to your arm. I like to call it arm candy for men.

7. A killer navy two-button suit – this is the first foundational piece that any aspiring professional needs. Navy is the professional dress code of Corporate America and not viewed as offensive or flashy. Avoid the patterns until you have a good rotation of suits.

8. A stunning gray two-button suit with a ticket pocket & side vents – this is a compliment to any setting. It can be light or medium gray. This works in any setting and pairs nicely with any color combination on the approved list (see #5).

9. A wool overcoat- this is a nice to have if you purchase year round or tropical wool suits. It completes the look for going to the office or date night.

10. A brown leather belt – this is necessary because it should match all of the brown shoes that you are going to purchase from tip #2!

11. A pair of dark straight leg jeans – this is a classic take on "dress" jeans. They should not have any holes, rips, tears, and should fit your silhouette but not too tight. Can easily be paired with a sport-coat or blazer for a "sporty" look.

12. A white silk pocket square – this is a classic staple because white matches everything! I suggest white because it fills the breast pocket of your coat without being obtrusive. Once you gain your confidence, branch out with colors, patterns, and textures.

3- THE START LIST

This chapter includes tips on what a man should do to elevate himself to the gentleman status. The list includes practical everyday things that can be added to your routine. Some of the tips can be done immediately, while others will require practice, and money.

Top 10 list of things that a true gentleman must START doing:

1. Start going to a tailor when you purchase clothing! Not everything on the rack will fit your body perfectly. Remember that clothes from the rack are made to a generic specification to fit the masses. I have everything that I own tailored because I like to feel good in what I wear. For instance, have your shirts taken in on the sides so you do not have the excess bagginess of your shirt.

2. Start rotating your shoes! I know you have a favorite pair of shoes, but you need to give them a break! Remember that quality shoes have leather bottoms and they wear out. Prolong the life of your shoes by letting them air out and use shoe trees to absorb moisture, retain the shape, and absorb moisture. Rotating your shoes adds variety and a little spice to your appearance.

3. Start purchasing less, but then better quality! Quality garments will last you longer. Save until you can purchase quality instead of the cheaper version that will have to be replaced later. I found this out the hard way… I settled for a cheap version of a cashmere sweater that I wanted for a while and it turned out to be a bad purchase. The sweater shed on everything that I had near it and the material was thin. I spent the money on the better quality sweater and I still own it to this day (11 years later).

4. Start shining your shoes each week! Just as you groom yourself, groom your shoes. Leather needs care just like skin! Shoes are the first things that people notice on a gentleman. Leave a good impression and give them something to remember you for…. This was a life lesson that my father instilled in me…he always taught me that shoes can make or break your entire look.

5. Start using shoetrees in your shoe collection! – A shoe tree prolongs the life of your shoes, absorbs moisture, and maintains the shape. Every shoe in my arsenal has a shoe tree even my slippers!

6. Start paying attention to your body type! Just because it is in your size does not mean it will look good on you. Always look for items that flatter your figure. I am a bigger guy and learned that I have to try on everything before I leave the store because the "fit" model does not match my proportions. I have a linebacker's build with wide shoulders, so I have to find things that accommodate my wingspan and fitting my waist. The textbook shape of the "perfect" man is a V, wider shoulders, and smaller waist...while I am not a perfect V; my body silhouette is wider at the top and trimmer at the waist. Some guys are an inverted triangle, narrow in the shoulders and wider through the waist. Spend more time looking at yourself in the mirror to find your "problem" areas for the proper fit.

7. Start dry-cleaning your shirts <u>without</u> starch! Starch is a shirts enemy because it will gradually breakdown the fibers and wear out the shirt. The shirt will look just as crisp without starch and gives a softer appearance versus the stiffness & sheen of starch. When I began working in after college, I was excited that I could afford to send my shirts to the cleaners, I asked for heavy starch in everything, my shirts could stand on their own and I never had to iron them. The thing that I did not realize is that the starch never came out and the shirts were prone to scorch marks from the iron. Imagine wearing a cardboard box to work! Now that I do not have starch added to my shirts, they drape and look natural on my body. I use a light iron in between cleaning to keep the wrinkles at bay.

8. Start a skincare/grooming regimen (manicure, pedicure, clean-shaven)! The myth that no one cares about a man's hygiene is not true, no one wants to look at an Ogre. Your appearance speaks volumes about your character. Your face is your best asset in many cases. I have never been able to grow a beard but I have always had a goatee and mustache. There are differing schools of thought on facial hair in a professional setting. Sometimes I shave off my moustache but never my goatee. It is a personal preference but just make sure it is neat and maintained.

9. Start having confidence! Having confidence makes you appear more competent and self-aware. Do not confuse this with arrogance...feeling good in your clothing requires practice and once it is mastered you can own your look and the room.

10. Start with a look and make it your own! Style is not something that you can purchase off the shelf! Look at the different trends and fits for your body type for cues on what to wear. I am not a big fan of white shirts but I know that I must own a few. I picked white shirts with texture and tone on tone patterns to make it more my style. I figured if I had to have one, why not elevate the level of sophistication.

4- THE STOP LIST

This chapter will focus on things that a gentleman should stop doing while building your wardrobe. These tips can range from how to button suits, things not to purchase, or coordinating looks.

Top 10 list of things that a true gentleman must STOP doing:

1. Stop purchasing square toe shoes! Pay attention to the shape of your toe box. Opt for something classic and timeless! Square toe shoes are reminiscent of the 1990's.

2. Stop purchasing cheap items period! No matter what kind of deal you can get it will not be worth it, in the end. Remember Quality over Quantity!

3. Stop purchasing the rainbow of shirt colors! This is not the circus…. build a wardrobe that can last for years and be paired with different accessories. Everyone wants to be noticed but not for the wrong reasons.. Know your environment and the unspoken dress code for your work life.

4. Stop thinking that you can never dress well; it is a mindset, persona, and act of confidence to dressing well

5. Stop thinking that everything on the rack is made for you!

6. Stop wearing rubber soled shoes with your suits! Rubber soles denote casual!

7. Stop buttoning up all the buttons on your suit jackets! Rule of thumb… if it is 2 button, only the top button is fastened; if it is 3 button, only the top 2 or the middle should be buttoned!

8. Stop wearing the same dress shoe every day! Spice up your outfits with a variety of shoes to show that you know how to mix and match a few things.

9. Stop wearing reversible belts! Remember that every time you fasten the belt on one side it leaves an impression on the other side of the leather....There is nothing worse than looking at the torn leather protruding through the hole on the other side of the belt.

10. Stop purchasing trendy professional clothing! Ever wonder why you are constantly purchasing work clothes???? Perhaps you have been purchasing what is in season versus timeless staples that never go out of style. I have gotten to a point in my life that if I can not wear it to work, I can not purchase it. I carefully select interchangeable items that can be worn at work and out in the evening. Remember the tip on Mastering Versatility...

5- THE SHOP LIST

This chapter will outline places to shop while building your wardrobe. The first thing that a gentleman must do is get measured by a tailor to find out your body type and size. Knowing what fits you well will be key to finding a store that caters to your size. Not all stores are alike!

Be aware of trends and remember that the current fad might not always work for your body type. Fit is the most important aspect of finding a place to shop. Many times, you will not be able to go into a store and purchase directly off the rack unless you are built like a "picture model". Let us face the facts that the average guy is not built this way.

To combat this problem, many stores offer made to measure clothing, which is made on a common pattern with small modifications to fit your size and body type. This is the best way to go if you can never find anything in the store that fits you. This is a little more expensive than purchasing off the rack, but you are ensured a good fit once you find the "right" brand.

If you have more money to dedicate to building your wardrobe, consider bespoke (custom) clothing. Bespoke is where all of your body measurements are captured, and a pattern is made specifically for you. By using the custom option, is the only way to ensure that the article of clothing was made for you. By far, Bespoke is the most expensive option because the garment is made by hand, which requires more man-hours to produce.

If neither the made to measure nor bespoke are options for your budget, find a good tailor to take the pieces that you find on the rack. Almost every piece of clothing that I own has been taken to a tailor for minor modifications. Shirts are the most modified piece of clothing in my closet. I love the look of a fitted shirt that tapers at the waist and follows the contours of my body.

Remember, develop your sense of style, and find stores that compliment your body type, price range, and desires!

6- THE SHOE LIST

The purpose of this chapter is to provide some context for all of the different types of shoes that are available in the market. The list will range from casual to formal with definitions for everything. Enjoy!

1. The straight-tip oxford – The toe (or front) of the shoe is cut or crafted straight. The oxford is typically considered the most formal shoe that a gentleman can own. Occasions such as weddings or funerals are appropriate, and the color is always black. This is equivalent to the little black dress that a woman owns. It is just something you have to own!

2. The whole cut – This is considered the quintessential formal shoe made from a single piece of leather. I love this shoe because it can be worn with a suit, trousers, sportcoat, and with a pair of dark jeans. Versatility at its best. I always opt for a shade of brown in this shoe because brown is the new black.

3. The plain toe oxford – Considered a universal shoe in your arsenal because of its understated plain toe. Any shade of brown works well! This pairs well with suits and sportcoats....

4. The wing tip oxford – Always classic and can be used from casual to formal with a wing shaped cap on the toe with perforations. I love to add a little interest on the toe box of my shoe and the wingtip is the perfect way to accomplish this. It gives me a sense of classic and refined. I recently purchased a pair in gray with a burnished (process of applying another color to the heel and toe of the shoe) black toe and heel for a little interest.

5. The plain toe derby – Casual or understated class at its best. These can be found in a variety of leathers, suede, with rubber and leather soles depending on the formality. This is a perfect shoe for dress down Friday's or casual days at the office.

6. The monk-strap – Coined after a type of shoe that monks would typically wear. Can go from casual to dress depending on the sole and type of leather. They also are made with a single or double strap in both shoes and boots. A great addition to any shoe collection. This is my all time favorite because it reminds me of the gents I saw while visiting London.

7. The Chukka boot – Hits right at the ankle for a casual look. Typically has a rubber sole with different variations in leather and suede. This is appropriate for weekend wear with some cords or jeans. Play around with color here....

8. The Loafer – A comfortable slip on shoe for your casual outfits and occasions. Made in a variety of leathers and suede with leather or rubber soles. Another favorite for casual and dress down Friday at the office.

7- THE SUIT LIST

The purpose of this chapter is to provide some context on all of the different types of suits and cuts that are available in the market. The list will range from classic to formal with definitions for everything. Enjoy!

1. The one button – This suit is commonly known in the "tuxedo" industry because of its simple nature and understated button placement. This model has become popular in business or professional suits because of the unusual nature. This look requires confidence!

2. The two button – The most versatile and classic suit made. It can be used for business to formal depending on the color and fabric choice. Elevate this suit with a ticket pocket and side vents.

3. The three button – The three button suit was popular in the late 1990s and early 2000s. Typically only the middle button should be buttoned or the top two. This model can also be made with side vents.

4. The double breast – Not for the faint at heart but those that exude their sense of style. The classic form features six buttons and side vents. The style can be elevated with a ticket pocket for a more English look. A classic staple in your closet.

5. The three piece – Typically worn on formal occasions, this suit features a waistcoat made out of the same fabric as the suit. The coat is typically a two button with side vents. This look can go from day to evening, depending on the confidence that you possess in pulling off the look.

6. The English cut– Coined after riding coats worn by jockeys. This cut features side vents, flap pockets, and a more fitted waist.

7. The Italian cut – This cut features a padded shoulder, slash pockets (no flaps), and no vent in the back.

8. The American cut – This cut features a slightly padded shoulder, slash, or flap pockets, vent or ventless back. This is what you will typically find in your major department stores.

8- THE SHIRT LIST

The purpose of this chapter is to provide some context for all of
the different types of shirts, collars, and cuffs that are available in
the market. The list will range from classic to formal with
definitions for everything. Enjoy!

Collars

1. Spread – The collar is slightly spread, which requires a wider knot.

2. Cut away – this is one of the extreme spreads. Commonly seen in British fashion. Requires a wider knot to make it look classy.

3. Classic Point – This is considered to be the "go to" collar style for the American man.

4. Button down – Considered to the most casual of the collars. Typically worn with casual outfits. The proper gentleman should never wear this with a suit!

5. Wingtip – Always classic and can be used from casual to formal with a wing shaped cap on the toe with perforations.

6. Club – This is a "throwback" to the 50's with a more tailored round look. Can be worn if you have enough "style" sense.

7. Contrast– Coined after the color contrast with the shirt and the collar. Typically, the collar is done in white to make a more formal look for a patterned shirt. Using contrasting fabrics has become very popular with casual shirts by mixing patterns, colors, and textures.

Cuffs

1. Single button – This is the most common cuff you will see for the ready to wear category.

2. Two button – This cuff features two buttons stacked on the cuff. This is becoming more common in ready to wear.

3. French cuff – the most formal of all of the cuffs. Features holes for those "eye-catching" cufflinks in your collection. Adds a little sophistication to any outfit.

4. Barrel – this cuff can have straight or rounded edges and comes in one and two buttons.

5. Mitered - this cuff features a cut away edge of the cuff and comes in one and two buttons.

9- THE TRAVEL LIST

This chapter will provide some tips that I have grown to love when traveling on business. Some are common sense, and others are a little more technical, but remember it is never too late to learn, change, or adopt a new regimen!

Top 10 list of travel tips for the true gentleman:

1. Always fold your suits! Folding suits helps to keep the fabric from wrinkling during travel. Numerous tutorials online show different folding techniques.

2. Coordinate all outfits on a business trip so that you take one pair of dress shoes, casual shoes, and perhaps an athletic shoe. The goal is to go from the office to dinner without packing your closet. Pair items that compliment and look good dressed up or down.

3. Always roll your undergarments and socks! Rolling takes up less space than folding. Once these items are rolled, you can use packing cubes or place them in your shoes for space maximization. If you remember tip #5 from The Start List, this will not work because your shoes will have a shoe tree!

4. Always fold your dress shirts! Folding your dress shirts maximizes space and minimizes wrinkling.

5. Always store your shoes in dust covers! Storing your shoes with dust covers (shoe bags) keeps delicate leathers and suede from becoming soiled. Think of covering your 65 Mustang in the garage…my shoes are equally as important!

6. Always keep a toiletry bag packed in your suitcase! If you are a frequent business traveler, this is necessary so you always have what you need and ready to go at the last minute.

7. Always pack a pair of dark jeans! This elevates your business casual dinner with a little bit of style. Pair it with your sportcoat and dress shirt for an upscale look.

8. Always have a backup belt!

9. Always pack a few days before a trip! Ease the stress of traveling by planning and ensuring that you do not forget anything.

10. Always think ahead and plan!

10- THE IMAGE LIST

This final chapter is dedicated to those who value the concept and art of dressing. The phrase "imagine is everything" is a bit cliché, it is true and more people should adopt this stance. As a young boy, I watched my father shine is dress shoes and work boots every week. He was trained in the military that imagine was paramount, and this was instilled in me. My father was a machinist by trade, which was a dirty and oily job, but he always made sure his uniform was ironed and his work boots had a mirror shine.

The notion of dressing for how you want to be perceived versus what type of job you have, has been forever imprinted in my core being. Oscar Wilde said it best, "You can never be overdressed or overeducated". Perception is something that everyone gets multiple shots at getting it right. I am not saying that first impressions do not matter, rather I am emphasizing that EVERYTHING can change because perceptions are fluid. They may not change overnight, but they can change with effort.

Do not let your "brand" be tarnished by your physical appearance or image. Dressing well gives you confidence versus arrogance, wit versus sarcasm, and humility versus pride if you understand why you get dressed every day. If you are dressing well for compliments versus building your "brand", you are doing it for the wrong reason. Have you ever admired what someone was wearing and thought, "Gee I wish I looked that way?" Was it their confidence, intellect, outfit, shoes, or their persona that made you look?

My philosophy is, just because they make it to fit you does not mean it is appropriate or a good fit for you!

ABOUT THE AUTHOR

Dr. Eduardo Haynes has a rich history of over 19 years in financial services with IBM, Wachovia, Bank of America, Edward Jones, and over 10 years in higher education beginning with Shaw University & University of Phoenix. Currently, he is a School of Business Faculty member for the Charlotte Campus for University of Phoenix and a Research Affiliate for the School of Advanced Studies at UOPX, as well. A graduate of the School of Advanced Studies at University of Phoenix, he holds a Doctorate in business administration, an MBA from the Goldbold School of Business at Gardner-Webb University, and a BS in business from North Carolina State University.

Active in the community, Haynes is the current Board Chair of Project One Scholarship Fund & the Mooresville Community Alliance, and was a member of the Mooresville Grade School District Business Advisory Council & the United Way of Lake Norman. He has also served on the Big Brothers Big Sisters Leadership Council and Impact Fund for the Foundation for the Carolinas.

Most recently, he was inducted into the 4th & 5th Editions of Who's Who Black Charlotte and named the 2013 North Carolina Distinguished Faculty of the Year, 2008 Faculty of the Month, and 2008 Faculty of Excellence for the University of Phoenix. In 2011, Eduardo received the prestigious Ted Jones Prospecting Award, which is awarded to new financial advisors in the first year of service by establishing 120 client relationships or more. In addition, Haynes was awarded the Pioneer Award, named in honor of Zeke McIntyre, which recognizes new financial advisors who achieve high levels of success early in their careers with Edward Jones.

Lastly, Haynes was inducted into the Gardner-Webb's Gallery of Distinguished Alumni for 2010, which the holds in high regard outstanding alumni and friends who demonstrate the values upon which Gardner-Webb was founded and who help to shape our local and global communities while serving to inspire current and prospective students. Through this initiative, the University recognizes and honors alumni and friends who have made significant contributions to their field of service and in the communities in which they serve. Haynes also was the recipient of the Gold, Silver, Bronze & President's Volunteer Service Awards from Bank of America. In 2007, Haynes was named one of the most influential African-Americans in the Charlotte area by WSOC-TV.

www.ingramcontent.com/pod-product-compliance
Lightning Source LLC
Chambersburg PA
CBHW050756290526
45792CB00008B/2202